GROWING F
F.

Comprehensive Guide To Rhododendrons Flower Care Tips And Techniques

FRANK BOBBY

Copyright © 2023 By Frank Bobby...

Please note that you must obtain explicit written consent from the publisher before reproducing, disseminating, or transmitting any part of this publication.

This applies to all methods, including photocopying, recording, or any other electronic or mechanical means. It's important to note that short excerpts that are smoothly integrated into reviews and noncommercial applications allowed by copyright law might not be subject to this restriction.

All Rights Reserved.

Table of Contents

Introductory 5
CHAPTER ONE 9
   Species And Variety Diversity 9
   Botanical Essentials 13
CHAPTER TWO 20
   Choosing The Appropriate Rhododendron 20
   Creating A Productive Growing Environment 26
CHAPTER THREE 34
   Planting Strategies 34
   Irrigation And Irrigation 42
CHAPTER FOUR 50
   Agriculture And Nutrition 50
   Reduction And Forming 56
CHAPTER FIVE 64
   Pest And Disease Control 64
   Propagation Techniques 71
CHAPTER SIX 77

- Container-Based Culture 77
- Winterization And Cold Protection 83

CHAPTER SEVEN 90
- Common Problems And Resolutions....90
- Conclusion..98

THE END...103

Introductory

Rhododendrons are a type of flowering plant that correspond to the Rhododendron genus, which consists of numerous species and cultivars. These flowers are renowned for their brilliant and multicolored blooms.

The significance of Rhododendron flowers varies according to cultural, historical, and individual interpretations. They are frequently associated with the following symbolic connotations:

• Elegance and Charm: Rhododendron flowers are admired for their remarkable beauty and vivid hues, which makes them a symbol of elegance and charm.

- The impressive appearance of Rhododendron blossoms is associated with admiration and appreciation. They may be bestowed in recognition of a person's qualities or achievements.

- In some cultures, it is believed that Rhododendron flowers offer protection against negative energies and evil entities. This symbolism may derive from their robust appearance and the concept of protection.

- Rhododendrons, like many other flowers, can be used to express a variety of emotions, including affection, gratitude, and even sympathy, depending on the context and the relationship between the giver and receiver.

- The intricate shapes and lush foliage of Rhododendron flowers can elicit a sense of mystery and intrigue. This may be due to their stealthy appearance and ability to merge in with natural landscapes.

- Due to the presence of toxic compounds in their leaves and flowers, some cultures interpret Rhododendron flowers as an indication of caution or a warning. This symbolism functions as a reminder of the possible dangers concealed by their beauty.

It's essential to note that flower meanings can vary widely across cultures and personal interpretations. Moreover, the significance of Rhododendron flowers may vary depending on the context in which they are given or used. Consider the recipient's cultural background and preferences if you are contemplating using flowers to convey a specific message.

CHAPTER ONE
Species And Variety Diversity

The Rhododendron genus is extremely diverse, containing numerous species and cultivars. These plants are well-known for their beautiful flowers and varied foliage, and they can be found in a variety of habitats around the globe. Here are some examples of the genus Rhododendron's diversity:

• There are over 1,000 different species of Rhododendron, and they vary in size, shape, color, and habitat. Some species are tiny, dense shrubs, while others are capable of developing into large trees. Each species has distinct characteristics and cultivation requirements.

- Rhododendrons can be found in numerous regions of the globe, including Asia, Europe, North America, and Africa. The Himalayas and other mountainous regions of Asia contain the greatest diversity of species.

- Rhododendron flowers are available in a broad range of hues, from pure white and pale pink to deep red, purple, orange, and yellow. They can be solitary or double, with tubular, bell-shaped, or flat flower shapes.

- In addition to their lovely flowers, Rhododendrons are frequently valued for their evergreen foliage. Leaves can be glossy or matte and appear in a variety of green hues. Additionally, some species have intriguing leaf textures and shapes.

- Numerous hybrid and cultivar varieties of Rhododendron have been developed by horticulturists and cultivators. These hybrids are frequently bred to exhibit specific characteristics, such as disease resistance, distinct flower colors, or varied growth patterns.

- Rhododendrons can flourish in a diversity of habitats, ranging from temperate forests to alpine meadows. Others are tolerant of slightly more alkaline soils.

• Despite the fact that the majority of Rhododendron species are ubiquitous and unthreatened, some are endangered due to habitat loss, climate change, and other factors. Important conservation initiatives are required to preserve the species diversity of this genus.

Due to the extensive diversity within the Rhododendron genus, a plethora of information about specific species and varieties is available. Whether you're interested in growing

Rhododendrons in your garden, studying their ecology, or simply appreciating their beauty, this diverse group of plants offers a variety of avenues to investigate.

Botanical Essentials

Here is an introduction to botanical concepts and terms:

1. Botanic Anatomy:

• Roots: Anchoring structures that absorb water and nutrients from the soil.

• Stems: Supporting structures that transport water, nutrients, and sugars from the roots to the foliage.

- Leaves are photosynthetic organelles that convert sunlight into energy.

- Flowers: Reproductive structures that generate spores via fertilization.

Fruits are structures that develop from pollinated blossoms and contain seeds.

2. Plant Expansion:

- Germination: The process whereby a seed begins to develop into a new plant.

- Vegetative Development: The development of stems, leaves, and roots prior to flowering.

- Reproductive Growth: The phase of plant development during which flowers, fruits, and seeds are produced.

- Senescence: The withering process of plant tissues that ultimately results in their demise.

3. The process of photosynthesis:

- The process by which plants use light, carbon dioxide, and water to produce carbohydrates (glucose) and oxygen.

4. Plant Procreation:

- Asexual Reproduction: Reproduction that occurs without the use of seeds or fertilization. To illustrate, consider runners, bulbs, and cuttings.

- Sexual Reproduction: Reproduction involving the formation of embryos through male and female reproductive cell fertilization.

5. The taxonomy:

- The study of identifying and classifying organisms. Kingdom, division (or phylum), class, order, family, genus, and species comprise the hierarchy.

6. Botanical Nomincombining:

- The system of designating plants using Latin or Latinized names, consisting of a capitalized genus name and a lowercase species name.

7. Botanical Physiology:

- The study of plant physiology, including growth, photosynthesis, water absorption.

8. Botanical Ecology:

- The study of the interactions between plants and their

surroundings, including other organisms and physical factors such as soil and climate.

9. Plant Evolution:

- Specific traits that aid plant survival and growth in their respective environments. Examples include the water-saving characteristics of desert plants and the ability of aquatic plants to survive in waterlogged conditions.

10. Naturalistic Gardens:

- Areas devoted to the cultivation, display, and conservation of diverse plant species, typically organized according to their geographical or taxonomic relationships.

11. Anthropological botany:

- The study of the relationship between plants and humans, including the traditional applications of plants in various cultures.

These ideas provide a foundation for comprehending the world of botany. Consider delving deeper into each topic and gaining hands-on experience with flora through gardening or fieldwork if you wish to learn more.

CHAPTER TWO
Choosing The Appropriate Rhododendron

Choosing the ideal Rhododendron for your garden requires taking into account a number of factors to ensure the plant's success in its new environment. Here are some essential considerations:

- Rhododendrons have varying climate and hardiness zone requirements. Ensure that the species or variety you select is appropriate for your climate and within the recommended hardiness zone for your region.

- Different species of Rhododendron have differing light requirements. Some flourish in complete shade, while others can tolerate greater sun exposure. Consider the illumination conditions in your garden when selecting an appropriate plant species.

- Rhododendrons favor acidic soil with a pH between 4.5 and 6.0. Determine the pH of your soil and choose plants that are compatible with it. If your soil is not naturally acidic, you may need to modify it in order to produce the appropriate conditions.

- Rhododendrons prefer soils with excellent drainage. They cannot tolerate wet environments. To prevent root rot, ensure that the planting site has adequate drainage.

- Size at Maturity: Consider the available space for your garden. Some varieties of Rhododendron can grow quite enormous, while others stay more compact. Choose a dimension that complements the layout of your garden.

- Flower Color and Form: Rhododendrons are available in a variety of flower colors and forms. Choose hues that complement your garden's existing design or that invoke a particular mood or aesthetic.

• Various varieties bloom at various times of year. Choose plants with bloom times that correspond with your intended garden aesthetic.

• Some Rhododendron varieties are more resistant to prevalent diseases than others. If you want to reduce maintenance efforts, investigate disease-resistant varieties.

• Choose Rhododendron varieties that can withstand freezing temperatures if you reside in an area with harsh winters.

- Consult local nurseries, gardening organizations, or horticultural experts in your area for advice. They can provide recommendations based on the conditions in your region.

- Consider the quantity of care you are willing to provide for the property. Some varieties may require more care in terms of pruning, fertilization, and insect control than others.

- Look for Rhododendron varieties that are resistant to the most prevalent pests and diseases in your region. This can help reduce the frequency of treatments required.

• Choose a Rhododendron that you find aesthetically pleasing and that complements your horticulture philosophy.

Keep in mind that, despite the fact that Rhododendrons are typically resilient and adaptable, proper planting and maintenance are essential to their success.

Prepare the planting hole thoroughly, amend the soil if necessary, and irrigate and mulch appropriately. By contemplating these factors and conducting research, you can choose a Rhododendron that will flourish in your garden and add aesthetic value to your outdoor space.

Creating A Productive Growing Environment

The success of your Rhododendron plants depends on your ability to provide them with the optimal developing conditions. Here are measures to take to create their ideal environment:

1. Select the Appropriate Location:

• Choose a location that receives the correct quantity of sunlight for the

Rhododendron variety you've selected. Others prefer partial shade, while some favor complete shadow.

• Ensure that the site has adequate airflow to prevent fungal diseases.

2. Rhododendrons prefer soil with a pH between 4.5 and 6.0. Determine the pH of your soil and adjust it as necessary.

• Create a permeable, well-draining soil structure by incorporating organic matter such as compost or well-rotted pine bark to enhance soil drainage.

3. Positioning Hole:

• Dig a planting trench that is twice as wide but not deeper than the root ball. To prevent water accumulation, the tip of the root ball should be slightly raised above the soil.

• If your soil is heavy or clayey, construct a shallow depression similar to a saucer around the plant to aid in water drainage.

4. Modifying Soil:

• Before filling the planting pit, incorporate organic matter such as compost, peat moss, or well-rotted pine bark into the backfill soil. This improves the structure and acidity of the soil.

5. The act of planting:

• Carefully remove the Rhododendron from its container and position it in the hole for planting.

• Fill the cavity with the amended soil mixture, ensuring that the plant is at the appropriate height.

• Water the soil generously to consolidate it around the roots.

6. Apply a layer of organic mulch around the plant's base, such as wood particles or pine needles. This aids in soil moisture retention, temperature regulation, and vegetation suppression.

7. The act of watering:

- Maintain the soil consistently hydrated, but not saturated. The shallow roots of rhododendrons make them susceptible to arid stress.

- Water profoundly and infrequently as opposed to shallowly and frequently.

8. To fertilize:

- Fertilize early spring and after flowering with a slow-release, balanced fertilizer formulated for acid-loving plants. Follow the instructions on the packaging for application rates.

9. During pruning:

• Regularly prune diseased or diseased-free branches to the plant's health.

• After flowering, prune lightly to shape the plant and promote bushier growth.

10. Insect and Disease Control:

• Keep an eye out for parasites such as aphids, scale insects, and caterpillars. Use as necessary.

- Avoid overhead watering, as damp foliage can encourage the growth of fungi.

11. Winter Security:

- In colder regions, apply a layer of mulch around the plant's base in the autumn to prevent the roots from chilling.

- To protect plants from harsh winter gusts, consider using burlap or a windbreak.

12. Regular servicing:

- Regularly inspect your Rhododendron plants for indications of stress, pests, and diseases. Prompt action can help prevent problems from escalating further.

Remember that each Rhododendron variety may have specific care requirements, so it is essential to research the demands of the particular type you are cultivating. Your Rhododendrons can flourish and bring years of beauty to your garden if you provide them with the appropriate care and attention.

CHAPTER THREE
Planting Strategies

To ensure that your Rhododendron plants establish themselves and flourish in their new environment, it is essential to employ proper planting methods. Here is a step-by-step planting guide for Rhododendrons:

1. Select the Right Moment:

• Typically, the best time to plant Rhododendrons is in early spring or early autumn, when the weather is mild and the plants have ample time to establish roots before extreme temperatures.

2. Gather Your Equipment:

- You will need a shovel, a trowel, organic matter or compost, foliage, water, and the Rhododendron plant itself.

3. Site Readiness:

- Choose a location that is well-drained and receives the right quantity of sunlight for your Rhododendron variety.

- Remove any weeds, grass, or detritus from the area.

4. Creating the Holes:

- Dig a trench that is twice as wide but not deeper than the root ball.

- To prevent water accumulation, the tip of the root ball should be slightly above the surrounding soil level.

5. Modifying the Soil:

- Mix organic matter like compost, peat moss, or well-rotted pine bark into the soil you removed from the cavity. This improves the structure and acidity of the soil.

- If the soil is dense or compact, create a shallow depression resembling a saucer around the plant to enhance drainage.

6. To plant a Rhododendron:

• Remove the Rhododendron from its container with care. If the roots are circling the root ball, separate them with gentle manipulation.

• Place the plant in the cavity with the top of the root ball slightly higher than the surrounding soil level.

• Fill the cavity with the amended soil mixture and pat it down to remove any air pockets.

7. The act of watering:

- After planting, water the plant vigorously to settle the soil around the roots.

- Maintain consistent soil moisture, particularly during the period of establishment.

8. Spread a layer of organic mulch around the plant's base, taking care to avoid the stem.

- Mulch aids in soil moisture retention, temperature regulation, and vegetation suppression.

9. Staking (if needed):

- If the Rhododendron is top-heavy or in a windy location, temporary staking may be required until the plant develops robust roots.

10. Planting Aftercare:

- Regularly inspect the plant for indicators of stress, pests, or diseases.

- Fertilize in the spring and after flowering with a balanced, slow-release fertilizer, per package instructions.

11. Watering Schedule:

• Maintain consistent soil moisture without allowing it to become waterlogged, particularly during the first growing season.

• Water thoroughly and infrequently to promote deep root development.

12. During pruning:

• After flowering, lightly prune the plant to shape it and promote bushier growth.

• Remove diseased or rotting branches as necessary.

By adhering to these planting techniques, you can give your Rhododendron plants a solid start and provide them with optimal conditions for robust growth and abundant blooming.

Irrigation And Irrigation

For the health and vitality of your Rhododendron plants, proper hydration and irrigation are required. Here are some guidelines for effectively watering your Rhododendrons:

1. Establishing a Routine for Watering:

- Water your Rhododendrons frequently and thoroughly, particularly in their first year after planting. This promotes the growth of a robust root system.

- Watering requirements may vary based on climate, soil type, and plant type.

2. Irrigation Frequency:

- Strive to maintain a consistently saturated, but not soggy, soil. Rhododendrons prefer soil that is mildly moist.

- Regularly test the soil's moisture content by inserting your finger about an inch into the soil. If the soil at this depth feels dry, it is time to irrigate.

3. Hour of the day:

• Water your Rhododendrons early in the morning or late in the day. Avoid watering during the warmest part of the day to reduce evaporation-related water loss.

4. Watering Strategies:

• Water the plant's base while avoiding the foliage. Wet vegetation can result in fungal diseases.

• Directly irrigate the soil using a soaker hose, drip irrigation system, or watering can with a fine nozzle.

5. Watering Quantity:

• Supply sufficient water to thoroughly saturate the root zone. A slow, thorough watering that reaches 6 to 8 inches deep is generally effective.

• Modify the quantity of water according to soil drainage and weather conditions.

6. Mulching Advantages:

• Spread a layer of organic mulch around the plant's base. Mulch aids in soil moisture retention, plant suppression, and temperature regulation.

7. Avoid Over-Irrigation:

• Excessive watering can cause root rot and other plant maladies. Ensure adequate drainage and water only when the soil exhibits evidence of drying out.

8. Adjusting for Precipitation:

• During periods of consistent precipitation, it may be necessary to reduce or suspend your irrigation schedule. In contrast, you may need to water more frequently during dry periods.

9. Adapting to Seasonal Variations:

- Seasonally, Rhododendrons have varying water requirements. They require more water during their active growing season and less water during their dormant period in the winter.

10. Surveillance of Plant Health:

- Observe signs of overwatering (wilting despite moist soil) and underwatering (wilting and desiccated soil). Adapt your irrigation practices accordingly.

11. Drip Watering:

- The installation of a trickle irrigation system can provide consistent and targeted watering, which is advantageous for maintaining soil moisture without wasting water.

Keep in mind that the irrigation needs of your Rhododendron plants will vary depending on climate, soil, and plant size.

Observing your plants and adjusting your irrigation schedule as necessary will ensure their health and well-being. Monitoring your Rhododendrons frequently and adjusting to changing conditions will allow you to provide them with the optimal amount of water.

CHAPTER FOUR
Agriculture And Nutrition

Fertilization and appropriate nutrition are essential for promoting healthy growth and vibrant flowering in Rhododendron plants. Here is a suggested approach to fertilization:

1. Understanding Dietary Requirements:

- Rhododendrons are acid-loving plants that necessitate particular nutrients for optimal growth. Nitrogen (N), phosphorus (P), and potassium (K) are the principal nutrients.

2. Selecting the Appropriate Fertilizer:

- Employ a balanced, slow-release fertilizer formulated specifically for acid-loving plants. Consider fertilizers with an N-P-K ratio close to 10-5-5 or 12-6-6, as these ratios are optimal for Rhododendrons.

3. Fertilization Scheduling:

- Fertilize your Rhododendrons in early spring, just prior to the onset of new growth. Fertilizing in late summer or autumn can stimulate new growth that may not have sufficient time to harden before winter.

4. Application Procedure:

- Evenly distribute the granular fertilizer around the plant's base, avoiding direct contact with the stem.

- Water the plant after fertilizer application to facilitate dissolution and root zone penetration.

5. The dosage:

- Follow the manufacturer's recommendations for the amount of fertilizer to use per plant. Overfertilization can result in nutrient imbalances and other complications.

6. Natural Fertilizers:

- You can also provide nutrients with organic fertilizers such as well-composted manure, fish emulsion, or cottonseed meal. These fertilizers gradually release nutrients as they decompose.

7. Small elements:

- Certain Rhododendrons thrive with trace elements such as iron and magnesium. Consider applying a fertilizer containing these elements if you observe yellowed leaves with green veins (chlorosis).

8. Consideration of pH:

• Rhododendrons prefer soil that is mildly acidic. If the soil pH is too high, certain nutrients may be difficult for the plant to assimilate. Determine the soil's pH and adjust it as necessary.

9. Reproduction Frequency:

• In most cases, a single application of fertilizer in the spring is adequate. Avoid over-fertilization, as superfluous nutrients are detrimental to the plant.

10. Mulching Advantages:

• As organic materials such as pine needles, wood chips, and bark decompose, they can progressively release nutrients into the soil.

11. Visual Perception:

• Monitor your Rhododendrons' foliage and overall growth. Consider modifying your fertilization strategy if you observe signs of nutrient deficiency, such as yellowing leaves or slow growth.

12. Balanced Method:

• Remember that while fertilization is essential for the health of your plants, a suitable growing environment, proper watering, and overall care are equally important.

You can ensure that your Rhododendron plants flourish and produce beautiful flowers year after year by fertilizing them and maintaining healthy soil conditions.

Reduction And Forming

Pruning and shaping your Rhododendron plants is necessary for maintaining their health, fostering good airflow, regulating their size, and enhancing their overall appearance.

Here are some guidelines for pruning and shaping:

1. The timing:

• Rhododendrons should be pruned after they cease blooming in spring. This allows you to appreciate the flowers while preserving the flower buds for the following year.

2. Tools:

• Clean and precise pruning shears or loppers should be used. This helps prevent plant damage and fosters clean, faster-healing wounds.

3. Planning for the future:

• Deadhead withered flowers by removing them from the plant. This encourages the plant to focus its energy on new growth as opposed to germ production.

4. Eliminating Deceased or Infected Wood:

• Inspect your Rhododendron for branches that are diseased, damaged, or deceased. Cut them back to healthy wood using precise incisions.

5. Shaping and Reduction:

- To shape the plant, prune branches selectively to maintain a desirable form. This may entail removing overgrown or intersecting branches.

- Thin out dense growth to increase ventilation, which reduces the likelihood of fungal diseases.

6. Renovation Pruning:

- Consider renewal pruning if your Rhododendron has become lanky or unruly. This is accomplished by cutting one-third of the eldest stems to the ground, thereby encouraging new growth from the base.

7. Cut Headings:

- Heading cuts (cuts that remove only a portion of a stem) should be avoided because they can result in unsightly regrowth. Instead, make precise incisions just above a leaf node or branch lateral.

8. After Severe Winter Damage, Prune:

- If winter damage occurs to your Rhododendron, wait until new growth emerges in the spring before assessing and pruning damaged areas.

9. Pruning Species versus Hybrids:

• Distinct hybrids and species may have distinct growth habits and requirements. Research the specific pruning requirements of your Rhododendron variety.

10. Back up and Observe:

• Periodically assess the shape and health of your Rhododendron from a distance. This helps you determine which areas require pruning.

11. Avoid Extreme Pruning:

- Rhododendrons have a natural form, and excessive pruning can be detrimental to their health and attractiveness. Pruning with restraint, removing only what is necessary.

12. Eliminate Removed Material:

- Properly discard pruned branches to prevent the spread of diseases. Do not compost plant material that is infected.

Remember that although pruning is essential, excessive pruning or improper techniques can cause plant stress. If you are uncertain about how to prune your specific Rhododendron variety, consult gardening guides, local experts, or professional landscapers to ensure the health and beauty of your plants.

CHAPTER FIVE
Pest And Disease Control

Management of pests and diseases is an essential aspect of caring for Rhododendron plants. Vigilance and prompt action can aid in the prevention and resolution of potential issues. Here is how to manage pests and diseases effectively:

1. Preventive measures:

• Choose Resistant Varieties: When selecting Rhododendron varieties, prioritize those renowned for their resistance to local pests and diseases.

Provide optimal growing conditions, including proper soil drainage, adequate sunlight, and consistent irrigation. Plants that are healthy are better able to resist parasites and diseases.

• Sanitation: Maintain a clean garden by removing fallen leaves, debris, and decaying plant matter, which can harbor pests and diseases.

• Good Air Circulation: Plant Rhododendrons with adequate spacing to promote good air circulation and reduce the probability of fungal disease.

2. Pest Control:

• Inspect Regularly: Inspect your Rhododendrons on a regular basis for signs of pest infestation, such as nibbled leaves, distorted growth, and visible insects.

• Physical Removal: If you observe a limited number of pests, you can physically eliminate them.

Use horticultural oil sprays to suffocate and control pests with delicate bodies, such as aphids and scale insects.

• Insecticide Soap: Insecticide detergents are effective against aphids, mealybugs, and spider mites. Observe the label's instructions attentively.

Encourage natural predators that prey on common garden pests, such as ladybugs and lacewings.

3. Disease Administration:

- Proper irrigation: Excessive irrigation can result in fungal diseases. Irrigate the plant's base while avoiding the foliage.

- Prune Diseased Material: To prevent the spread of fungal spores, promptly remove and dispose of any diseased leaves or branches.

- Fungicide Treatment: In the case of persistent fungal diseases, fungicides may be required. Consult with a nearby horticulture center or extension service for pertinent advice.

- Maintain proper spacing, adequate air circulation, and avoid overhead watering to minimize conditions conducive to fungal diseases.

4. IPM (Integrated Pest Management):

- Integrated Pest Management (IPM) is an approach that incorporates multiple strategies for managing pests and diseases. It emphasizes pesticide prevention, monitoring, and minimal use.

- Identify the insect or disease, evaluate the problem's severity, and select the most appropriate control measures based on the specific situation.

- IPM often involves using a combination of cultural practices, biological controls, and targeted pesticide applications as a last resort.

5. Professional Assistance:

- If you are uncertain about the identification or management of a particular pest or disease, consult with local horticulture experts, extension services, or professional landscapers.

Remember that prevention and early intervention are essential to the successful management of pests and diseases. Regular monitoring, appropriate cultural practices, and a proactive approach will help maintain the health and vitality of your Rhododendrons.

Propagation Techniques

Numerous methods exist for propagating Rhododendrons into new plants. Here are some common methods of propagation:

1. Seed Reproduction:

• Although Rhododendrons can be grown from seeds, this method is typically sluggish and unreliable due to hybrid genetic variations.

• Collect seeds from mature seedpods in the autumn and sow them in well-draining, acidic potting mix in a seed tray or container.

- Maintain consistent moisture and indirect light around the seedlings.

- Germination can occur anywhere from several weeks to several months. Once seedlings have reached the appropriate size, they can be transferred to larger containers or planted directly in the garden.

2. Reduced Propagation:

- Rhododendrons are commonly and effectively propagated from cuttings.

- Take softwood or semi-hardwood cuttings in the spring or early summer from robust, disease-free plants.

• Soak the cut end of the cutting in rooting hormone and position it in an acidic, well-draining rooting medium-filled container.

• Place the container in a moist environment and apply bottom heat to promote rooting.

• Once the cuttings have developed roots, they can be potted up and grown on until they are suitable for planting in the garden.

3. The use of multiple layers:

- Layering is the process of encouraging a stem to develop roots while still attached to the parent plant.

- Select a low, bendable branch and bring it to the ground.

- Create a tiny incision on the underside of the branch and bury it in the ground, securing it with a stake or rock.

- Roots should form at the site of injury. Once the young plant has established roots, it can be severed from the parent and transplanted.

4. The procedure of grafting:

• Grafting is the process of attaching a scion (desired plant variety) to a rootstock (a distinct Rhododendron plant).

• This method is frequently used to propagate difficult-to-root varieties from cuttings.

• The scion and rootstock are joined and secured using a compatible grafting technique (such as whip-and-tongue grafting).

• The new plant can be grown once the graft union has cured.

Success in propagation can vary depending on the Rhododendron variety and technique used. Certain types of Rhododendrons and hybrids are better adapted to particular techniques. Experimenting with various techniques and gaining knowledge from seasoned cultivators or horticultural resources can aid in successful propagation.

CHAPTER SIX
Container-Based Culture

If you have limited garden space or specific growing requirements, growing Rhododendrons in containers is an excellent way to appreciate these beautiful plants. Here's how to cultivate Rhododendrons in containers successfully:

1. Select the Appropriate Container:

• Choose a large, durable container with adequate drainage openings. Rhododendrons have shallow root systems, so a receptacle that is both wide and shallow is ideal.

- Use a container with a diameter of at least 18 to 24 inches (45 to 60 cm) to allow for adequate root development.

2. Choose the Appropriate Rhododendron Varietal:

- Select varieties of Rhododendron that are suitable for container cultivation. Compact or dwarf variants are advantageous.

3. Growing Medium:

- Use a well-draining, acidic potting mixture formulated specifically for acid-loving plants such as Rhododendrons and Azaleas.

• Organic matter, such as peat moss, can be added to the mixture to increase acidity and moisture retention.

4. The act of planting:

• Fill the container with a layer of potting soil. Remove the Rhododendron from its nursery pot with care and position it in the container at the same depth as it was in the original pot.

• Fill the voids with potting soil and pat it gingerly around the plant.

5. The act of watering:

After planting, you must thoroughly water the plant to consolidate the soil. Maintain consistent moisture levels, preventing the soil from becoming either too wet or too dry.

6. Located at:

• Place the container in a location that provides the ideal light conditions for the particular Rhododendron variety. Some individuals may prefer partial shade, while others can tolerate more direct radiation.

7. To fertilize:

• Apply a slow-release, acid-loving plant fertilizer in the spring and after blossoming, per the instructions on the package.

8. Apply a thin layer of organic mulch to the surface of the container to aid in soil moisture retention and temperature regulation.

9. Trimming and Forming:

• Pruning and shaping the Rhododendron on a regular basis will help maintain its compact growth habit. Remove any diseased or rotting branches.

10. Observe the plant for signs of stress, insects, and diseases. Regularly check the soil's moisture content and modify your watering schedule accordingly.

11. Containerized Rhododendrons are more susceptible to cold temperatures. During the winter, it may be necessary to move the container to a protected location or to wrap it in burlap.

12. Consider repotting your Rhododendron every few years into a slightly larger container with new potting soil. This enables the plant to continue to thrive in its growth.

You can create a stunning display on terraces, balconies, and in small gardens by cultivating Rhododendrons in containers. You can appreciate the beauty of these plants in a confined space by providing the right growing conditions, regular maintenance, and proper care.

Winterization And Cold Protection

Providing cold protection and overwintering Rhododendron plants is essential, particularly if you live in a region with severe winters.

Your Rhododendrons will survive and flourish in the spring if they are cared for properly during the winter months. Here is how to protect your Rhododendrons from the cold:

1. Choose Frost-Tough Varieties:

- Choose Rhododendron varieties that are adapted to your climate and can withstand the cold in your region.

2. Irrigation Prior to Winter:

- Water your Rhododendrons thoroughly before the ground freezes in the autumn. Moist soil helps prevent winter desiccation.

3. Apply an organic mulch layer around the base of the plants to insulate the soil and protect the roots from frigid temperatures.

4. Wind Shielding:

- Excessive winter winds can dehydrate and injure Rhododendron leaves. Consider using burlap or other materials to construct a windbreak to shield the plants from harsh gusts.

5. Anti-Dampness Sprays:

- Apply anti-desiccant treatments to the foliage prior to winter's arrival. These sprays create a protective coating that aids in preventing the loss of moisture through the leaves.

6. Finishschütt:

• Burlap can be wrapped around plants in colder regions to provide additional insulation and protection from freezing gusts. Ensure that the top is left uncovered for air circulation.

7. Security for Containers:

• If you are growing Rhododendrons in containers, move the containers to a sheltered location, such as a garage or a corner of your property that is shielded from the wind. To prevent chilling, insulate the containers with straw or bubble wrap.

8. Anti-Permeability Agents:

• By forming a thin, protective coating, anti-transpirant sprays can reduce water loss through the foliage. Follow the product's application instructions.

9. During pruning:

• Avoid excessive pruning in the autumn because it can stimulate new growth that may not have sufficient time to harden before winter. Instead, prune after flowering in the spring.

10. Observe Moisture:

• During times when the ground is not frozen, examine the soil's moisture content to ensure that it is neither too wet nor too dry. Watering the soil when it is malleable prevents root stress.

11. Protection against snow:

• A layer of snow provides vegetation with insulation. Leave a thin layer of snow on your Rhododendrons if feasible, rather than brushing it off.

12. Check for Damage:

• Monitor your Rhododendrons for signs of damage, such as fractured branches or frost damage, after severe weather.

Keep in mind that different Rhododendron varieties may have differing weather tolerances. By providing adequate protection, you can secure the health of your Rhododendrons during the winter months and encourage their growth in the spring.

CHAPTER SEVEN
Common Problems And Resolutions

Rhododendrons are susceptible to a variety of health and aesthetic issues. Early identification of these problems and application of the appropriate solutions can help your plants thrive. Here are some typical problems and their solutions:

1. Leaves Turning Yellow (Chlorosis):

• Yellow leaves with green veins indicate a deficiency in a nutrient, typically iron or magnesium.

• Adjust the pH of the soil to make nutrients more accessible. You can treat the deficiency with iron chelates or a fertilizer with micronutrients.

2. Fallen Leaves:

- The wilting of leaves despite a moist soil may indicate root rot due to inadequate drainage or excessively humid conditions.

- Solution: Improve soil drainage, ensure appropriate watering methods, and, if necessary, consider transplanting to a better-draining location.

3. Diseases caused by fungi (Leaf Spot, Powdery Mildew, etc.):

- Issue: Fungi can produce discolored spots on leaves, powdery growth, and other atypical conditions.

- The solution is to remove and destroy infected leaves, increase air circulation, and refrain from overhead watering. In severe cases, fungicides may be required.

4. Insect pests (Aphids, Scale Insects, etc.):

Insects can harm leaves, alter plant growth, and impair plants.

• Solution: Conduct routine inspections, remove vermin manually if possible, introduce natural predators, and use insecticidal soaps or oils as necessary.

5. Winter Harm:

• Problem: cold temperatures and winter winds can result in leaf burn, discoloration, and branch damage.

• Provide wind protection, cover plants with burlap, and avoid late-season pruning that stimulates new growth.

6. Poor Florescence:

• Problem: Incorrect pruning, insufficient radiation, or poor nutrition can lead to a lack of or a reduction in flowering.

• Solution: Prune after flowering, ensure appropriate light conditions, and apply a balanced fertilizer formulated for acid-loving plants.

7. Root Problems:

• Problem: Rhododendrons with unhealthy root systems are susceptible to diminished growth and poor health.

- Solution: Ensure adequate drainage, avoid planting too deeply, and examine roots for symptoms of disease or damage prior to planting.

8. Excessive UV Radiation:

- Issue: When leaves are seared by intense sunlight, they can develop brown spots.

- Solution: Plant the Rhododendron in a location that receives sufficient sunlight for its variety. If required, provide afternoon shade.

9. The Big Game:

- Issue: Rhododendron foliage is susceptible to deer browsing, resulting in visible damage.

- Use deer-resistant fencing or repellents to prevent deer from consuming your vegetation.

10. Incorrect Pruning: - Problem: Incorrect pruning can result in misshapen or lanky growth. Learn appropriate pruning techniques and only prune as necessary to maintain the plant's natural form.

11. Newly planted Rhododendrons may experience distress as a result of their transplanting. - Solution:

Water the plant adequately before and after transplanting, as well as during the recovery period.

12. Nutrient Imbalances: - Problem: Imbalances in soil nutrients can effect the health and growth of plants as a whole. Conduct a soil analysis to ascertain nutrient levels, then amend the soil accordingly.

Identifying the precise problem influencing your Rhododendron is essential for employing the proper remedy. Regular monitoring, adequate care, and prompt intervention can help maintain the health and beauty of your plants.

Consider consulting local horticulture experts or extension services if you are uncertain about the issue.

Conclusion

Growing and caring for Rhododendrons can be a rewarding and satisfying endeavor, enabling you to take pleasure in their vibrant flowers and lush foliage.

You can create a flourishing garden or landscape by understanding the diverse species and varieties available, as well as the specific requirements of these plants.

Remember these essentials:

• Select varieties of Rhododendron that are well-suited to your climate, soil, and intended growing conditions.

• Site Preparation: Create an ideal growing environment with appropriate soil pH, drainage, and sunlight based on the requirements of the Rhododendron variety you've selected.

• Follow proper sowing techniques to ensure proper root establishment and development.

• irrigation and Irrigation: Maintain soil moisture without waterlogging with consistent and adequate irrigation.

• Fertilization and Nutrition: Provide your Rhododendrons with the proper nutrients to encourage healthy growth and blooming.

• Pruning and Shaping: Routinely prune and shape your plants to preserve their shape, health, and overall appearance.

• Management of Pests and Diseases Observe and resolve pests and diseases promptly to prevent plant damage.

• Overwintering and Cold Protection: Provide Rhododendrons

with winter care to protect them from severe weather.

• Container Cultivation: If you have limited space or specific needs, you can enjoy the majesty of Rhododendrons in containers.

By combining these techniques, you can cultivate a flourishing Rhododendron-filled garden. Remember that each variety may have specific needs, so observing your plants, learning from experience, and requesting advice from local gardening resources will contribute to your success.

Your Rhododendrons can bring years of joy and color to your outdoor spaces with the appropriate care and attention.

THE END

Printed in Great Britain
by Amazon